FAMILY MATTERS

You and an Illness in Your Family

Tabitha Wainwright

the rosen publishing group's
rosen central

Published in 2001 by The Rosen Publishing Group, Inc.
29 East 21st Street, New York, NY 10010

First Edition

Library of Congress Cataloging-in-Publication Data

Wainwright, Tabitha.
You and an illness in your family / Tabitha Wainwright. — 1st ed.
p. cm. — (Family matters)
Includes bibliographical references and index.
ISBN 0-8239-3352-0 (library binding)
1. Sick—Family relationships—Juvenile literature. 2. Family—Health and hygiene—Juvenile literature. [1. Sick.] I. Title. II. Series: Family matters (New York, N.Y.)
R130.5 .W35 2000
610—dc21

00-010035

Manufactured in the United States of America

Contents

You can share your feelings about an illness in your family with your friends.

Introduction

When dealing with illness in your family, whether it's life threatening or temporary, you may experience many new feelings. You may feel scared, worried, stressed, sad, or lonely. You may have to take on extra responsibilities and may have to adjust your schedule to meet the needs of your family. If your mother usually drives you to soccer practice and she is in the hospital, you will have to see if you can get a ride with a friend. If you live in a single-parent family and your father is bedridden with pneumonia, you and your siblings will have to prepare meals.

When a family member is sick, trying to figure out how to go about your day-to-day life can be very challenging. Though reading a book on this subject cannot make a sick person better, it can provide you with useful information that will help you understand what you are feeling and learn how to cope with these tough situations.

When a member of your family becomes ill, you may not know how to react.

1

Dealing with an Illness: The Stages

When a member of your family becomes ill, whether it is a parent, a grandparent, a brother or sister, or your cat or dog, you may not know how to react. If you know what to expect, you may have an easier time understanding this new situation. According to the National Coalition for Cancer Survivorship (NCCS), the first stage of dealing with an illness is finding out more information about the illness.

A Sudden Illness

When an illness shows itself suddenly—like a heart attack—it can be more of a shock than an illness that progresses slowly.

It was Leila's birthday, and she was on her way home from school. Her mom was having a big party for her. All her friends were coming over later to eat cake. When Leila turned the corner, she saw an ambulance with flashing red lights in her family's driveway.

"Oh, no," she said out loud. "What if it's Mom?"

Leila ran over to the ambulance. The first person she saw was Ms. Thompson, her neighbor and close family friend. When Ms. Thompson saw Leila, she took her aside and told her that there had been an accident, and her mother would be in the hospital for a while. Since Leila didn't have any family close by, she would have to stay with Ms. Thompson until her mother could come home.

Leila's mother's sudden illness—she had a heart attack and her left side was paralyzed—was very startling. After all, her mother had been fine in the morning. Leila couldn't believe it was true, even after she went to the hospital and saw her mother lying pale and weak in bed.

During her first few hospital visits, Leila would talk on and on, telling her mother how she wanted her to come home so that they could finish building a tree-house in the backyard. She told her mother that she didn't understand why she was still in the hospital. In fact, Leila seemed completely unaware that her inability to come to terms with the seriousness of her mother's situation was causing her mother stress.

Denial

Denial is when you are not able to accept the reality of a situation. This is a common reaction to a sudden illness. This was Leila's reaction—to deny that her mother's heart attack had even happened. In fact, Leila's mother and Ms. Thompson became concerned about Leila, because she was having such a hard time facing reality.

Denial is when you are unable to accept the reality of a situation, such as a parent's illness.

On behalf of Leila's mother, Ms. Thompson spoke to the hospital social worker who in turn sat down with Leila and went over a list of emotions that Leila would probably be experiencing, specifically denial, anger, confusion, fear, and guilt.

The Importance of Sharing Your Reaction to an Illness

Leila was relieved once she talked with the social worker. She had been very confused by the different feelings that she was experiencing. Rachel, the social worker, and Leila created a chart so that Leila could keep track of her feelings. The two met once a week t over the chart. Rachel described different s, and together they came up with definitions emotions. Then Leila would fill in the columns e name of the emotion that related to how she eeling.

After her weekly session with Rachel, Leila felt better. This is why it is very important to share your feelings. If you have a sick family member and you need to talk to someone, try talking to an older brother or sister, a close neighbor, another relative, or a teacher or counselor at school, or ask an older relative to contact a hotline or social worker with whom you can speak. You will find some useful addresses and phone numbers at the back of this book.

Understanding Emotions

It is important to understand that it is all right to experience a variety of confusing feelings. Even anger is a natural reaction to this kind of stressful situation. Don't feel guilty or mad at yourself if you are annoyed at your sick family member, or if you are mad because you are getting less attention than you usually do. Instead, allow yourself to feel angry (at least for a little while), and let someone who is close to you know that you are feeling this way. Once you acknowledge your emotions, you will feel better.

If you feel sad or lonely and you want to cry, don't be afraid that doing so will mean that you are weak. Crying is good for us. It allows us to release some of what we are feeling. Once you start expressing your emotions, and you

Chart for the Week of
December 1st to December 7th

A) Emotion: Denial
Definition: Inability to believe what is going on.
What I feel: I can't believe Mom is sick. It just can't be true. I don't get it. Maybe when I go back to the hospital tomorrow, she'll be fine.

B) Emotion: Anger
Definition: Being mad at the way things are.
What I feel: I'm mad that Mom is in the hospital and not at home with me. I'm mad I didn't get my party. I'm mad that my dad doesn't live in this country. I'm mad this is happening.

C) Emotion: Confusion
Definition: Inability to understand things.
What I feel: Sometimes I feel okay and then other times I feel really sorry for Mom. Sometimes I feel badly that I can go out and play and she has to stay in the hospital. My parents are divorced and Dad lives in France, and I don't know if I should call him since he and Mom don't get along well.

D) Emotion: Fear
Definition: Being scared; having a funny feeling in stomach.
What I feel: I want to cry a lot. What if Mom dies? What if I leave the stove on by mistake and I burn down the house? Where will I go?

E) Emotion: Guilt
Definition: Feeling bad about something.
What I feel: I feel bad that I still want my birthday party. I feel bad that I sometimes wish that my best friend's mother was in the hospital, too, so I wouldn't be alone.

Telling other people how you are feeling makes it easier to accept the reality of a situation.

let other people close to you know how you are feeling, it will be easier to move to the final step of dealing with an illness—acceptance.

When an Illness Is Gradual

You may react differently to an illness that does not occur suddenly. Unlike Leila, you may have a family member who has an illness that is slowly getting worse. If you are in this kind of situation, you may experience an even more confusing variety of emotions, and they may last for a longer period of time.

George's sister Isabella was born with only one lung. Since she was a baby, Isabella had always been very weak and the whole family had always been extra careful with her. When Isabella turned nine, her doctor suggested that she undergo a lung transplant so that she would finally have two working lungs. Since George was used to thinking of his sister as "sick," he didn't think much of the news of his sister's organ transplant. In fact, he didn't even know what it meant.

His parents, on the other hand, were extremely worried, and they become annoyed with George for being what they said was "insensitive." For a while, George went to his friend Daniel's house every day after school. He needed to get away from his crazy, spoiled sister and his annoying parents.

After he had shown up at Daniel's house five days in a row, Mrs. Matthews, Daniel's mom, asked him if anything was going on at home that he would like to talk about.

"It's awful, Mrs. Matthews. Everyone is being mean to me and it's just because Isabella is still sick and may have this transplant thing. They don't seem to care about me anymore at all."

"George," replied Mrs. Matthews, "of course they care about you. It's just that a transplant is a very serious and scary operation. Didn't anyone tell you what it involves?"

"No," replied George.

After that, George and Mrs. Matthews, who was a nurse, had a long talk about organ transplants

Communication is an important part of family life, but it is especially vital when a family member is ill.

and George's feelings. George felt relieved to know that his family didn't hate him. He now understood that they were just extra worried about Isabella, and that he had misunderstood the whole thing. He also realized that just as he was thinking that they no longer cared about him, perhaps his parents and sister were upset that he was spending all of his time at Daniel's house.

George didn't even stay at Daniel's house for dinner that night. He quickly went home to give his parents and sister a hug.

George's anger and confusion at how his family was reacting was due to the lack of information that was communicated to him about what was going on with his sister. George had not asked any questions and no one had taken the time to discuss the transplant procedure with him. At this point, if George were to have written a list of what he was feeling, it would have included the following:

- Anger
- Annoyance
- Frustration
- Betrayal
- Sadness
- Confusion
- Loneliness

That's a lot of emotions for one person. And a lot of them could have been avoided if George's family had worked more at communicating their feelings and explaining what Isabella was going through.

The Importance of Communication

Communication is an important part of all family matters, but it is especially vital in times of crisis, such as when a family member is ill. Unfortunately, during such emotional and stressful times, you may find that it is harder than usual to communicate with your family members. This is surely a difficult time for everyone involved. If you are having trouble communicating with a parent, sibling, or other family member, you may want to find someone outside of the family—such as a school counselor—who will listen and help you sort through your emotions.

When you find out that a family member is sick, you may want to have more of an understanding of what that person is going through. If a parent decides to shield you from the severity—or seriousness—of a situation, that is his or her choice. But you should feel free to ask questions.

Since doing research on your own can be confusing, and since inaccurate information is easy to come by if you look in the wrong places (some Internet sites post unauthorized information, for example), try asking a teacher, librarian, or older relative to direct you to good sources of information.

Ask a teacher, librarian, older relative, or other trusted adult to direct you to good sources of information about a particular illness or to listen to what you are feeling.

Knowledge can be powerful. If you have an understanding of what someone with an illness is going through, you will be better equipped to cope effectively with the situation. Not only will you know what to expect, but you will also be aware of how you can help the ill person in your family.

Anger is a natural reaction to the stress that comes with a family member's illness.

2

Changes in Your Life

Aside from learning how to deal with many new emotions, an illness can bring about other changes in your life. These kinds of changes depend on the severity of the illness and the particular structure of your home.

Putting Your Emotions to Work for You

With an ill family member at home or in the hospital, it is very likely that you may have less free time. This will especially be true if you live in a single-parent home, if you do not have any other siblings, or—in the case of a more serious illness—if most of your extended family members live far away.

Your first reaction to being told that you can't go out, or that you must come right home from school, will probably be anger. However, no matter how annoyed you feel, it is important that you also realize that now, more than usual, your family really needs your help. As we discussed in the previous chapter, it's natural to feel angry, but it's what you do with that anger that is important.

In this kind of situation, put your anger to work for you. When people become annoyed, they often get a rush of energy—called adrenaline. Use this adrenaline rush to help clean up the dishes, water the plants, pick up your younger brother from school, or make a nice card for whoever is in the hospital.

Asking for Help

Your family situation may be such that with one parent ill and the other working long hours, you and your brothers and sisters will have to take on a lot of extra work around the house. Perhaps you are an only child. Or maybe you live in a single-parent home and you have no other siblings or relatives who are close by. Families come in all sorts of sizes, and however your particular family is constructed, you may find yourself to be in a bit of a bind.

If this is the case, you may want to see if you can arrange for another relative or family friend to give you some help. If no one is available, ask a neighbor for help. It is important to remember that it is not bad to ask for help. Some people find it very difficult and embarrassing, especially if you need to ask for help from someone that you don't know very well. In these situations, remember that for the most part, people are a compassionate and caring bunch. Most people are happy to help.

If it still makes you feel uncomfortable to ask a neighbor to drive you to a store or to help you change a lightbulb, you can always offer to return the favor.

You could set up a system by which you keep track of what the neighbor (or friend) has helped you with, and you could suggest doing any of the following for them:

- Mow or rake the lawn and water plants
- Feed and/or walk pets
- Baby-sit
- Help with grocery shopping
- Return movies to the video store
- Take back library books

Time Management and Dividing the Workload

If your mother or father is sick, and you have a brother or sister who can help you, it's best to divide up the extra housework or chores that you may have. You may want to write out a schedule and put it somewhere where you can see it easily. If you cooperate with each other and take turns

Don't be afraid to ask for help from neighbors. You can return the favor by running errands for them.

cooking meals or helping to buy groceries, you will still be able to spend time doing the things that you normally do, like hanging out with your friends and riding your bike.

Since doing extra housework is not the most fun thing in the world, and since dividing up the extra tasks may be kind of stressful, you might want to change this process into a fun activity, as outlined on the next page. This way, you will take the emphasis off the negative—doing more work and deciding who will clean the toilets—and focus on the positive side—working together to make your household run more smoothly.

If you do end up making charts, you may want to keep them to show to your ill parent or relative. Your mother or father will be very impressed with your excellent organizational skills. (And you don't have to tell them that you got the idea from a book.)

When a Sibling Is Sick: "It's Not Fair"

If your brother or sister is ill, whether he or she is at home or at the hospital, you may feel different about helping out than you would if a parent were ill. Don't be surprised if you feel angry, resentful, lonely, or frustrated.

First of all, you'll be happy to know that it is not unusual to feel this way. Second of all, it is normal to feel a bit of resentment. Many people experience a different set of emotions when a brother or sister is sick. This is because you have a very different relationship with your siblings than you do with your parent or parents.

The Task Hat

What You Will Need

- A hat
- Paper
- Pens
- Scissors
- A coin
- A colored piece of cardboard paper
- A magnet

Preparation

- Make a list of the tasks that need to get done.
- Write each task on a separate slip of paper. Fold each slip of paper in half.
- Put all slips of paper into the hat.

How to Play

- Flip a coin to see who will pick first from the hat.
- The first player picks a slip from the Task Hat. Then the second player picks a slip from the hat. This continues until the Task Hat is empty.
- Open each slip and read what is written on it.
- At this point, if you want to trade tasks, you can.
- Make a schedule. Write the days of the week on the colored piece of cardboard paper and write down who will be doing each chore on a particular day.
- Secure the schedule to the refrigerator with a magnet.

Unlike how you feel about your parent, you may think of your brother or sister as an equal. If he or she is ill and therefore doesn't have to make his or her bed or clean the bathroom, you may feel that you don't need to do these things either. This is where your emotions become more complicated and you might find yourself regressing—or reverting back to how you behaved when you were younger. We regress when we feel that our needs are not being met. This is why, although you want to be mature and help out, you may find yourself acting childish, resenting all of the attention that your sick brother or sister is getting.

Just to prove that regression is normal and that you are not the only one who feels jealous or left out, take a look at the quotes below. These quotes come from kids who were asked how they felt when they had a sick brother or sister.

When I was ten, my little sister, Sage, broke both her ankles in a skiing accident. Every day people came over after school to sign her casts. She was allowed to talk on the phone way more than I was and Mom even let her play video games. In fact, the video games were moved into her room, and I never had time to play since I had to water all of the plants and help Mom cook dinner.

I felt really bad until I talked to Aunt May, my mom's sister. Aunt May told me that Mom felt that Sage's accident was her fault since she gave her permission to go on the class ski trip. After that I realized that my Mom was really worried about Sage. I guess my childish behavior wasn't helping.

Anyway, Aunt May told Mom how I was feeling, and the next day Mom gave me a hug as soon as I came home from school. She told me she was really glad I was around to help. She said that when Sage got better, she was going to take me to the ballet to thank me for doing so much stuff around the house.

—Elissa, thirteen, Cincinnati, OH

Tell your parent if a sibling's illness is causing you to feel neglected.

I have a twin brother and he was in the hospital for a year because his school bus was in an accident and he was in a coma for a long time. I felt bad for him but I was mad that all of our teachers at school kept calling me by his name. And our friends would call the house and ask how Glenn was doing before they would ask to speak to me. The worst was when Natasha, a girl at school who I really like, asked if she could go visit Glenn. And she had never said a word

Ask your parent for attention if you are feeling lonely or underappreciated.

to him before the accident! It was as if no one knew I even existed. I felt really awful and I even stopped doing my homework since my teachers didn't seem to care. I didn't even go to the hospital to see Glenn since just thinking of him made me mad.

After I moped around gloomily for a few weeks, my dad asked me what was wrong. He had assumed that I was worried about Glenn, but I told him that I felt like everyone liked Glenn better than me and I was the one who should have been in the coma. Dad looked really surprised to hear me say all of that. He explained that people were really concerned about Glenn and that it wasn't a question of people liking him better.

After that, I started to go to the hospital every other day to visit Glenn.

—Eric, twelve, St. Paul, MN

While it is okay to regress for a while, now is the time when your parents will really need to count on you. Let them know how you feel, and then remind yourself that being sick isn't a treat. Your sick sibling isn't having any fun with chicken pox or pneumonia. If you are feeling that you are doing all sorts of extra work and no one is paying any attention to you, don't be afraid to let your parents know how you are feeling.

If you don't feel comfortable telling your parents that you are feeling left out, try writing a note. Some people find it easier to express themselves in writing. A simple "I miss you" or "Mom, I wish I could see more of you" can do a lot. Or tell another relative or family friend how you are feeling. Maybe he or she could pass the information on to your parent or parents.

If you have tried several of these methods and your needs still are not being met, you may want to speak to a school counselor. In some cases, parents can become easily overwhelmed and may not respond well to the extra stress and pressure involved in caring for a sick child. If you are being neglected—if you are being left alone overnight, if there is no food in the house—you will need to get help. This is when you definitely should speak to a guidance counselor or a school social worker.

When a family member is ill, you and your siblings will probably have to be a lot more self-reliant.

Taking Care of Yourself

3

When someone in your family is ill, it may happen that for a while, you are more on your own than usual. You may have less access to your parents or other siblings since you will all be chipping in and trying to help out. In this case, you will have to be even more responsible than usual. If this is a scary thought, don't be alarmed. Remember that you are a very resourceful person.

After all, look at all that you have been able to do while your parent, brother, sister, or other close relative has been out of commission. You have helped to organize how and when extra chores need to get done, and you have spoken up for yourself when you've needed information about your family member's illness or when you've wanted to remind your parent or parents that you need attention, too. All in all, you have been a great help to everyone.

However, while you have been busy helping out and being mature, responsible, and a wonder-kid, you have to make certain that you are not neglecting yourself.

Here are some examples of what kids in your situation have done to take care of themselves.

When my mother was sick, I was basically on my own. She was in the hospital and then she would come back home for a week or so, and then she would go back in for more tests. I had no relatives close by, and since my mother wasn't working, we didn't have much money. I ended up going to a soup kitchen to get food, and then I had to drop out of school and get a job so that we could pay the rent and keep the apartment. At the time, I was only fourteen, so I got a job helping a tailor in his shop. But I was stressed out and I couldn't sleep. My mind would spin and I couldn't focus on anything. I needed to relax but I couldn't.

My English teacher and I were kind of friendly, and she called to find out what was going on. When I told her, she helped me fill out the forms for welfare so that I could quit the job and go back to school. She then told me about an afterschool program at the YMCA. I went there five days a week after school and played basketball. I met a lot of kids there who also didn't have a lot of money. They took turns inviting me over for dinner and to sleep over so I wouldn't be alone, or worse, so they wouldn't put me in a foster home. It went on like this for six

Always make sure to take care of yourself—participate in activities that you enjoy and spend time with people who can give you emotional support.

months, and then my mother got better and she came back home for good. Life is still kind of hard, but whenever I get stressed out, I shoot some hoops and all of my troubles seem to go away.

—Jerome, fifteen, Houston, TX

Dealing with Stress

Jerome found that playing basketball was a good way of dealing with the stresses involved in having a sick parent. You may not be a basketball enthusiast, but is there an activity you enjoy that relaxes you? Perhaps you like reading books or talking on the phone to friends. Think of a few activities that you like and make sure that you allow yourself some time to do things that give you pleasure.

While some stress can be a good thing, too much stress is bad for you. Stress is useful when it motivates you to get things done. But it is bad if it is getting in the way of you being able to function normally.

How do you know if you are under too much stress? Take a look at the questions below. If you answer "yes" to most of the following questions, chances are that you need some help managing your stress.

- Are you having difficulty sleeping?
- Have you experienced any changes in appetite—either eating a lot more or a lot less than usual?

- Do you find that your mind is racing from idea to idea and you are unable to concentrate?
- Are you having trouble enjoying the things that you usually take pleasure in?
- Are you experiencing unusual stomach pains or headaches?
- Do you feel more irritable than usual?
- Have people remarked to you that you are acting differently?

Stress can result in a lack of appetite or other changes to your normal routine.

You may be wondering how you can ask for help when your whole family is in turmoil. If you don't feel that you can voice your concerns to a parent or older relative, try talking to your school counselor, a teacher, or the parent of a good friend. If you really do not know where to go for help, there are associations and toll-free numbers you (or someone else) can contact. Take a look at the Where to Go for Help section at the back of this book.

Keeping Up with School

If you are going through a difficult time at home because of a family member's illness, you may want to notify your teacher of your current situation. Often an illness can get in the way of your having enough time to do homework. In addition, maybe you are not able to attend school every day. If this is the case, instead of keeping quiet while your grades drop and your teachers become annoyed with you for never being there, speak up. If you and your teachers work together, you will be able to make up an alternate schedule that will allow you to keep up with your classes. This is what Sharee did.

> *My dad was out of work and in the hospital because he had a heart attack, and my mom had to take on two jobs. Because of this, I needed to stay at home a few days a week to look after my younger brother and sister. Even though my mom told me to tell my teacher what was going on, I didn't because I was embarrassed. I missed lots of school and the band teacher kicked me out of the band.*
>
> *Then the principal called. My mom was the one who answered the phone, and she ended up spilling the beans. At first I was really mad at her, but Mr. Weir was nice and he talked to my band teacher and*

now I am back in the band and I am getting tutored so I can keep up with the rest of my classes.

No matter what you are going through at home, remember that school is important, too. Your teachers are there to help you learn, and most of the time, they will be understanding if you give them a chance and are open and honest with them.

Also, school can be a nice diversion from what's going on at home. Don't forget that you have your friends there, and going to class will give you the chance to take your mind off feeling sad or worried.

Whenever possible, you should prepare yourself emotionally for the death of a loved one or family pet.

When the Going Gets Really Tough: Fatal Illness

4

This last chapter deals with the really tough stuff—fatal illness. If words such as "fatal" and "terminal" are being used to describe your sick family member, you may want to start thinking about the fact that he or she may not be around forever. The idea of death and long-term illness is never easy to come to terms with. When hope runs out and it appears that your loved one, be it your father, mother, sister, or family cat, may not get better, you need to start preparing yourself for the harsh reality of death.

In these situations, denial (discussed in Chapter 1) can be hard to overcome. How are you supposed to get your mind around the fact that someone who you love dearly may never be the same again (in terms of terminal, debilitating illness), or may die soon? This book does not attempt to provide any answers, but we would like to mention some things to keep in mind if you and your family find yourselves in this situation.

Saying Good-bye

Throughout this book, the importance of communication has been stressed. With fatal illness and death in the picture, it is even more vital that you keep the communication lines open. Saying good-bye to a loved one is hard; in fact, it's more than hard. It may be one of the most difficult things you do in your life. And though it may seem easier to deny that death is an unavoidable fact, don't do it. You will regret it later on. Instead, think of a way to say good-bye to your loved one. This will provide closure (a sense of completion), and that will help you go on with your life. Here are some examples of how kids your age were able to achieve closure.

> *My cat was dying. We were going to put her to sleep in a week. I made sure we had nice photos of her, and I talked to her and told her how much I loved her. She had stopped purring a while ago, but the last time I picked her up, she purred. It was like she was saying good-bye to me, too. Now whenever I miss her, I look at her picture, and it's like she's still here.*
>
> *—Masako, thirteen, Iowa City, IA*

My brother was in a car crash. He wasn't going to come out of his coma. We didn't know how long he would live, but every time I went to visit him, before I left, I would always hold his hand and tell him he was my best friend. I did this every day for two months until the day he died. I'm glad I did it. It made it easier to let go.

—Ralph, fifteen, Los Angeles, CA

My mother had a disease called multiple sclerosis. She got worse and worse for years. We never knew when we would lose her. It made no sense to me. I was mad, and I couldn't believe she would go away forever. My dad took me to see his priest. Father Parsil made me feel better when he told me to pray for the soul of Mama so that God would hear me. Every night I said an extra prayer for Mama, and when she finally died, I put a photo of the two of us in her coffin. I know I'll always be with her and that God did what he thought was best.

—Rosaria, fourteen, Holbrook, AZ

When life gets really hard, remember that family matters. Your family will be yours for the rest of your life. When you cooperate and help each other through tough times, you'll come out stronger in the end.

Glossary

adrenaline Secretion of the adrenal glands, located above the kidneys, that causes a sudden increase in energy and physical strength.

coma State of prolonged and deep unconsciousness, usually caused by a serious head injury.

denial Refusal to admit the truth, or being unable to deal with the reality of a situation.

guilt Feelings of self-reproach for not behaving or acting in an appropriate way.

multiple sclerosis Disease of the nerve insulation in the brain and spinal cord.

organ transplant Surgical procedure where an organ (kidney, liver, heart, etc.) that is not functioning well is exchanged for one from a donor that is working better.

regress To revert to a past type of behavior; in particular, going back to behavior patterns of one's youth.

vital Necessary to maintain life.

Where to Go for Help

In the United States

American Cancer Society
1599 Clifton Road NE
Atlanta, GA 30329-4251
(800) 227-2345
Web site: http://www.cancer.org

American Self-Help Clearinghouse
St. Clare's Hospital
25 Pocono Road
Denville, NJ 07834
(973) 625-9565
Web site: http://www.mentalhelp.net/selfhelp

Big Brothers Big Sisters of America
230 North 13th Street
Philadelphia, PA 19107
(215) 567-7000
Web site: http://www.bbbsa.org

Families Anonymous
P.O. Box 3475
Culver City, CA 90231-3475
(800) 736-9805
Web site: http://www.familiesanonymous.org

Families with Children
Hospice of the North Shore
2821 Central Street
Evanston, IL 60201
(847) HOSPICE (467-7423)
Web site: http://www.carecenter.org/services/bereavement.html

National Mental Health Association
Information Center
1021 Prince Street
Alexandria, VA 22314-2971
(800) 969-NMHA (6642)
(703) 684-7722
Web site: http://www.nmha.org

In Canada

Boys and Girls Club of Canada
7100 Woodbine Avenue, Suite 405
Markham, ON L3R 5J2
(905) 639-0461

Canadian Cancer Society
10 Alcorn Avenue, Suite 200
Toronto, ON M4V 3B1
(888) 939-3333
Web site: http://www.cancer.ca

Canadian Mental Health Association
2160 Yonge Street, Third Floor
Toronto, ON M4S 2Z3
(416) 484-7750
Web site: http://www.cmha.ca

Canadian Red Cross Society
1430 Blair Place
Gloucester, ON K1J 1G2
(613) 740-1900
Web site: http://www.redcross.ca

Canadian Traumatic Stress Network
3727 Trans-Canada Highway, RR#1

Tappen, BC VOE 2XO
(250) 835-4473
Web site: http://www.ctsn-rcst.ca

Web Sites

Adolescence Directory On-line
http://education.indiana.edu/cas/adol/adol.html

Band-Aides and Blackboards
http://funrsc.fairfield.edu/~jfleitas/contents.html

Bereavement and Hospice Support Netline
http://www.ubalt.edu/www/bereavement

Teen Advice Online
http://www.teenadvice.org

For Further Reading

Appleton, Michael and Todd Henschell. *At Home with Terminal Illness: A Family Guide to Hospice in the Home.* Englewood Cliffs, NJ: Prentice Hall, 1995.

Bluebond-Langner. *In the Shadow of Illness: Parents and Siblings of the Chronically Ill Child.* Princeton, NJ: Princeton University Press, 1996.

Buckman, Robert, M.D. *What You Really Need to Know About Cancer: A Comprehensive Guide for Patients and Their Families.* Baltimore, MD: Johns Hopkins University Press, 1997.

LeShan, Eda J. *Learning to Say Good-Bye: When a Parent Dies.* New York: Macmillan, 1976.

Newman, Susan. *Don't Be S.A.D.: A Teenage Guide to Handling Stress, Anxiety and Depression.* Englewood Cliffs, NJ: Silver Burdett Press, 1991.

Packer, Alex J. *Bringing up Parents: The Teenager's Handbook.* Minneapolis, MN: Free Spirit Publishing, 1992.

Silverstein, Alvin, Virginia Silverstein, and Laura Nunn. *Depression*. Springfield, NJ: Enslow Publishers, 1997.

Wilson, Antoine. *Family Matters: You and Death in the Family.* New York: Rosen Publishing Group, 2000.

Index

About the Author

Tabitha Wainwright has a degree in education as well as a master's degree in children's literature.

Photo Credits

Cover and interior shots by Ira Fox.

Design and Layout

Geri Giordano